Black and Gold Dynasty

The Championship History of the Pittsburgh Steelers

Book 2: Super Bowl X

By

Jason Zemcik

About the Author

Jason Zemcik is a lifelong Steelers, Penguins, and Pirates fan who was born and raised in Somerset, Pennsylvania. He has written and published multiple books about his favorite Pittsburgh teams as well as one about the Holly Springs (North Carolina) Salamanders Coastal Plain League baseball team, a collegiate summer league squad, and one about his hobby of collecting hockey jerseys.

His writing has also been featured on the Pittsburgh Post-Gazette website, CityofChampionsSports.com, and MLBCenter.com.

He currently lives outside of Raleigh, North Carolina with his wife and daughter.

You can connect with him on Facebook (@jasonzemcikauthor) and Twitter (@JasonZemcik) to stay up to date on all of his latest writing.

Also by Jason Zemcik

Pittsburgh Sports

Other Sports

Free Book!

Get the digital version of *Buc to Good: The Trials, Tribulations and Triumph of Being...and Staying... a Pittsburgh Pirates Fan Through the '90s and 2000's* free when you go to my website jasonzemcik.com and subscribe to my newsletter

Everyone knows the story on the surface. The Pittsburgh Pirates suffer a heartbreaking defeat in Game 7 of the 1992 National League Championship Series – the infamous Sid Bream game – and go on to plummet into what became the longest streak of consecutive losing seasons in major professional sports history before finally making it back to the playoffs in dramatic fashion in 2013.

But for the segment of folks who continued to identify themselves as Pirates fans throughout the two-decade journey to redemption, seeing their belief that winning baseball would again be played in Pittsburgh one day come to fruition represents an entirely different story. It's a story of perpetual optimism, of loyalty, and of loving a team like family.

Buc to Good: The Trials, Tribulations and Triumph of Being...and Staying...a Pittsburgh Pirates Fan Through the '90s and 2000's is the story of these fans, as told by one of them. From the low of the '92 NLCS loss, to the "didn't think it could get any worse" years that followed, to the euphoria of the '13 Wild Card Game, *Buc to Good* touches all the bases on each true Pirates fan's emotional ride to seeing their team return to prominence.

CONTENTS

Previously in the Black and Gold Dynasty Series

Book 1: Super Bowl IX

The 1974-75 Pittsburgh Steelers captured the franchise's first championship by defeating the Minnesota Vikings in Super Bowl IX, and in the process set the stage for one of the most remarkable dynasties in professional sports. Their history prior to that season, dating back over four decades, had been largely unsuccessful, with only a handful of winning seasons and fewer playoff appearances to their credit.

Bolstered by a crop of future Hall of Fame players in the likes of Greene, Bradshaw, Harris, Swann, Stallworth, Lambert, Ham, and Blount and led by coach Chuck Noll, who would also claim a spot in Canton, Ohio after his storied career ended with four Super Bowl victories, the Steelers exhibited a turnaround through the early 1970's but were still in search of a first title to legitimize their success.

The 1974-75 squad changed all of that, winning with both skill and tenacity and establishing a culture of Steelers pride that now spans multiple generations and touches fans everywhere from western Pennsylvania to the far reaches of the globe. That Steelers team was the foundation for all of the franchise's great accomplishments over the following years; the first champion in what would become a lasting legacy of success for the black and gold and a way of life for their fans.

Chapter 1 – "You Gotta Deal With Us Now"

There's an episode of the NFL Films series *A Football Life* where Joe Greene retrospectively describes the impact of the Steelers' Super Bowl IX victory in the simplest yet most profoundly resonating way. Greene's recollection sheds light not only on how the Steelers' first championship shaped the team's growth on the field but also what it meant for the entire city of Pittsburgh. He recounted the pride he felt in that 1974 squad putting the Steelers on the NFL map, in reversing the previously negative connotation that the franchise had carried with it for so long, by recalling that the victory was a message to all other teams in the league that "you gotta deal with us now."

For Pittsburghers, that message had an inspiring ring to it. "You gotta deal with us now." The Steelers. Their Steelers. No longer a non-contending doormat as they were since their inception, or a close-but-no-cigar runner up as they were in the playoffs of years prior. They were the champions, the kings of the NFL. They were the talk of Pittsburgh, and moreover they were the team that every other team in the NFL had to talk – and worry – about. The Steelers had arrived, and they weren't going anywhere any time soon.

But despite all the fanfare associated with winning, all the excitement over punctuating the transformation process by reaching the pinnacle of the sport, and all the bolstering of attitudes that a Super Bowl victory brought about, there was still one man who wasn't as much unimpressed by it all as he was level-headed about it. In other words, he was just the person the Steelers needed to guide them into the next phase of their evolution, the one where everyone would indeed be gunning to knock them from their pedestal.

Chuck Noll was a one-man library of insightful, no-nonsense ideas about how to approach work. He was full of wise musings that quite frankly could be applied to almost any aspect of life. He wasn't interested in motivating his players, famously contending that he'd rather fill his roster with professionals who could handle that part of their craft on their own. He was the epitome of an "act like you've been there before" coach, and held that the thrill in anything came from the doing, the process, and the journey as opposed to just the actual winning. So, when training camp opened in Latrobe to officially kick off the 1975 season, it wasn't lost on any of the Steelers that they'd better be ready for the bull's eye that came with being defending champions.

With their roster from the previous season still largely intact they were well-stocked for their title defense. The core nucleus of players on both sides of the football were back, and when the team reached an agreement with L.C. Greenwood on a new contract after his previously-agreed to deal with the World Football League fell through as the upstart circuit crumbled, the entire Steel Curtain front four was also set to return and continue wreaking havoc on opposing offenses. All told, the black and gold were primed and ready when training camp and the lengthy exhibition schedule finally drew to a close and the regular season was set to get underway.

As it turned out, primed and ready was actually a drastic understatement.

Just in case the Steelers' faithful felt like they didn't have enough opportunities to celebrate during the offseason, the team did their followers a favor when they took the field for the season opener in September. The Steelers headed west to kick off the campaign against the San Diego Chargers, and the game was, in a word, a trouncing. The final score of 37-0 Pittsburgh wasn't the only area where the numbers showed an extremely lopsided tilt in the Steelers' favor. They outgained San Diego on offense by a margin of nearly four to one, racking up over 440 yards and besting the Chargers in first downs 24-9. Quarterback Terry Bradshaw appeared to pick up right where he left off the previous year, tossing two touchdowns against no interceptions, while the defense forced four Chargers' turnovers. The Pittsburgh ground attack was balanced, accounting for nearly half of the offensive total despite Super Bowl IX Most Valuable Player Franco Harris notching only 75 yards rushing himself. Harris was complimented nicely by Rocky Bleier and Reggie Harrison, who combined for nearly 100 yards.

The fact that the Chargers went on to finish the season tied for the worst record in the NFL notwithstanding, the Steelers took care of business in the opener in a way that sent a message to the rest of the league that the road to the Super Bowl would indeed run through Pittsburgh that year. Or at least that was the external view. Within the four walls of the Steelers locker room, Noll preached a different message to keep his club focused. Shutout or not, he cautioned that they were in for a much more difficult test the following week when they faced the Buffalo Bills in their home opener, a rematch of the previous year's AFC divisional playoff contest.

The Buffalo team that came to Three Rivers the following Sunday looked like a very different squad than the one the Steelers had easily dismissed in that playoff matchup nine months earlier. Beneath a sunny and mild late summer Pittsburgh sky that was in stark contrast to the frigid December day of the earlier playoff tilt, the Bills ran roughshod over the defending champion Steelers 30-21. It was the type of game that wasn't nearly as close as the final score indicated, as Buffalo jumped out to a 23-0 lead and coasted to victory while the Steelers managed two fourth quarter touchdowns to make the score look respectable.

Largely to credit for the dominant Buffalo victory was running back O.J. Simpson. The Steelers' defense hardly enjoyed the same success that saw them stonewall Simpson in the previous year's playoff game. Simpson galloped for over 200 yards, 88 of them coming on a single touchdown run. The Steelers helped Buffalo out through their own missteps as well. Bradshaw completed only three of eight passes, tossed an interception, and also fumbled before being lifted in favor of backup Joe Gilliam in the third quarter. The offensive line allowed four sacks and the Steelers collectively turned the ball over five times on the afternoon. In short, they simply had no answer for the Bills that day, who clearly came to Pittsburgh with payback on their minds.

A humbling defeat on their home turf may have been exactly what the Steelers needed though. It clearly reiterated that as champions they were going to get every team's best effort, week in and week out. The early reality check that life at the top of the mountain was in many ways going to be tougher than the pursuit of getting there propelled the Steelers to a prolific remainder of the regular season in the months that followed. At the time though it simply made for one unhappy locker room afterward, not to mentioned a disappointed Three Rivers parking lot and plenty of upset living rooms as fans headed home or glumly turned off the broadcast in their own homes.

In the following week's game at Cleveland the Steelers displayed a renewed fire, a rekindled sense of championship swagger that led them to a convincing victory against their heated rivals to get back on track. Bradshaw exited the game early after sustaining a hand injury, but the offense didn't skip a beat when Gilliam came on in relief. Three different running backs, Harris, Mike Collier, and Harrison, all found the end zone. Gilliam tossed two touchdowns to go along with Bradshaw's one with Lynn Swann, John Stallworth, and Reggie Garrett the recipients as the offense put up 42 points. The defense allowed only one harmless fourth quarter Cleveland touchdown. The Browns missed the extra point to typify their miserable afternoon, setting the final at 42-6 Steelers.

The game is remembered by many though not as much for the lopsided score as it is for one of the most famous expressions of the Steelers' tenacity from that era. Feeling frustrated that in his estimation the Browns had been egregiously holding him throughout the game and getting away with it, Greene took matters into his own hands in the second quarter. A brawl erupted when Greene kicked and threw a Browns player to the ground, and the rival squads had it out on the field before order was restored. Greene was ejected and subsequently fined, but his message was clear – the Steelers weren't going to stand being messed with.

That mindset carried through the next two games, a 23-9 victory over the Denver Broncos and a 34-3 thumping of the Chicago Bears, both at Three Rivers. With the defense clearly exerting its dominance and the offense putting up prolific numbers, the Steelers were humming along in championship form after their awakening against the Bills.

The following week's opponent, the Green Bay Packers, provided a tougher test yet still couldn't stop the Steelers' machine. Nor could the blustery conditions in Milwaukee where the game was held as part of the Packers' annual practice of playing a select few games away from Lambeau field due to the support they received throughout the state of Wisconsin. Pittsburgh jumped out to a 13-6 lead by virtue of a Collier kickoff return for a touchdown and two Gerela field goals, but the Packers tied the game in the third quarter before another Gerela field goal in the fourth quarter helped the Steelers squeeze out a 16-13 victory.

Though they were 5-1 nearly halfway through the season, the Steelers' mark was only good enough for second place in their own division. Their opponent the following week, the Cincinnati Bengals, had navigated the first six games undefeated to sit atop the AFC Central standings. The teams' head to head meetings, both the immediately-looming one at Riverfront Stadium as well as the season's next-to-final contest to be held at Three Rivers, would be critical in deciding the division champion and guaranteed playoff representative. Knowing full well the implications of the contest, the Steelers arrived in Cincinnati on that first Sunday in November ready to play.

They surrendered an early field goal but dominated thereafter, jumping out to a 23-3 advantage as Bradshaw connected with Swann on two touchdown passes and Bleier found the end zone on the ground. The Bengals closed the gap in the third quarter but couldn't pull even, and the Steelers added another late score on their way to a 30-24 victory that brought them into a tie for first atop the Central. But even with one game of head to head advantage against the Bengals in the books, the Steelers still had plenty of work ahead of them. The surprise Houston Oilers had also started the season 6-1 and were neck and neck with Pittsburgh and Cincinnati. Fittingly enough, they were also the Steelers' next opponent.

With the advantage of home field the Steelers defeated the Oilers in that game, though victory didn't come easy. Greene was sidelined with an injury and did not play, but his teammates stepped up in his absence. The Steelers jumped out to a 10-0 lead but suffered a lapse in the second half, allowing Houston to tie the score at 17-17 in the fourth quarter. In the final minutes though the Steelers awakened again and mounted a game-winning drive that covered nearly 80 yards. Though simply getting into position for a Gerela field goal attempt was the original aim, Bradshaw found Stallworth open for a 21-yard touchdown pass that sealed the victory and propelled the Steelers into sole possession of first place and the inside track for a playoff berth.

But despite the tremendous boost from having beaten both of their chief competitors in consecutive weeks, the Steelers' work just to get to the playoffs was far from over. They defeated the 4-4 Kansas City Chiefs the following week in what could very well have been a classic letdown game, only to go right back into the fire by having to travel to Houston the following week to battle the Oilers again. The game brought with it an opportunity to all but eliminate at least one challenger from the divisional race though, and in front of a Monday Night Football national television audience the Steelers capitalized on that opportunity to an exponential degree.

The Houston team that challenged Pittsburgh the entire game just two weeks earlier was nowhere to be found in the Astrodome that night, despite a heavy dose of anticipation from the home crowd leading up to kickoff. Or perhaps playing on Monday and knowing that Cincinnati had been upset by Cleveland the day prior gave the Steelers even more incentive to elevate their play, as they could significantly widen their divisional advantage with a win.

Whatever the cause, it was a clinic in domination. The defense notched the first score on a safety in the opening quarter as defensive end Dwight White recovered an errant snap in the Oilers' end zone and didn't let up throughout the matchup. During the third quarter the Steelers held Houston without a first down, and in the fourth quarter cornerback Mel Blount intercepted a pass and galloped 45-yards on the return to set up a Pittsburgh touchdown that pushed the final score to 32-9. The win ran the Steelers' record to 9-1 on the season, and they were beginning to separate themselves from the 8-2 Bengals and 7-3 Oilers in the Central race.

But there was still plenty of work to be done. The following two games were also prime opportunities for a team coming off of a big win to fall victim to complacency, and the Steelers needed to look no further than the Bengals' misstep against one of those opponents, Cleveland, for proof. First up though came a trip to the Big Apple to face the New York Jets.

Though the Jets were struggling, carrying a record of 2-8 into the matchup, the Steelers were playing on a short week that included a lengthy travel itinerary. They would also be without Greene again. After missing the Kansas City game, their defensive leader returned for each of the previous two contests but was once more hampered by a pinched nerve and unable to suit up. The injury ultimately kept Greene out for the next several weeks, so the rest of the Pittsburgh defense needed to elevate its play to help fill his void as the Steelers mounted their charge toward the playoffs. Needless to say, despite the Jets' record a victory at Shea Stadium was hardly a foregone conclusion.

At least not leading up to the game. When Sunday arrived, the Steelers showed no signs of fatigue and no intention of letting off the gas pedal in the race to the playoffs. They continued the workmanlike streak they had been on of late, jumping out to a 20-0 lead through three quarters and cruising home with an easy 20-7 victory. Two Bradshaw touchdown passes, one a 44-yard catch and run by Harris, and two Gerela field goals more than did the job for the Steelers. Simultaneously that day in Cincinnati, the Bengals were in the process of defeating the Oilers. Cincinnati's victory coupled with another Houston loss meant the battle for the division was down to a two-horse race between the Bengals and Steelers, who were due to meet at Three Rivers two weeks later in a contest that would likely settle score.

But, while winning the Central division was of course the first order of business for the Steelers, there was another team that they were almost certainly keeping tabs on, even though nobody in the team circle would likely admit it, at least not publically. The Oakland Raiders were just a game off the Steelers' pace for the best overall record in the AFC at 9-2, their blemishes coming in back to back October loses to Kansas City and, of all teams, Cincinnati. Heading into the season many a football pundit predicted that the Steelers and Raiders were on a crash course to meet again for the AFC title, and while not overlooking the necessary work to get there, human nature dictated that there were thoughts tucked away in the minds of everyone in black and gold that finishing with a superior record to Oakland would mean home field advantage should that prediction indeed come true.

The Steelers took care of business the following week against Cleveland, though the win didn't come easily. With the temperature hovering right round the freezing mark at kickoff to fittingly usher in the first weekend of December, the Browns jumped out to an early lead and carried a 17-10 advantage to the locker room at halftime. The Steelers found their stride in the second half though, scoring three times and shutting out the Browns to claim a 31-17 victory. Bradshaw and Swann connected for two touchdowns through the air and Harris scored on the ground. That same afternoon on the other side of Pennsylvania, the Bengals handled the hapless Philadelphia Eagles 31-0, setting the stage for a dramatic battle in Pittsburgh the following weekend.

Knowing that they controlled their own destiny when they kicked off against the Bengals, the Steelers left nothing to chance. They scored on their first offensive possession when Bradshaw connected with Swann from the 3-yard line and followed by notching a defensive touchdown on the ensuing Bengals' possession as defensive back J.T. Thomas took a Jack Lambert lateral on a fumble return and reached the end zone. Harris also found the end zone in the first half, and the Steelers' point total at the break would have been enough to win the game as the defense clamped down in the final two quarters knowing the division title was all but in their grasp. The final score was 35-14 Steelers and, in some good news from across the country, the Oilers edged the Raiders 27-26. The two outcomes combined meant that Pittsburgh not only had claimed the AFC Central title but also would finish with the best record in the conference and have home field advantage throughout the playoffs.

The victory also meant that the following week's game, the regular season finale at Los Angeles, was entirely meaningless for the Steelers. The Rams however had quite a bit on the line, as a win coupled with a Minnesota loss would give Los Angeles the top overall NFC record and home field throughout the playoffs. Those two factors led to an outcome that was hardly surprising, as the Rams defeated the Steelers 10-3.

If anything, ending with a loss after reeling off eleven straight wins helped bring the season back into perspective for the Steelers. Not that it had escaped them, but simply to serve as a reminder that in the NFL wins don't come easily, and in the playoffs they're even harder to obtain. As the post season commenced, the target that they had worn all season as defending champions was about to get even bigger, and the stakes for each game even steeper. The Steelers had successfully completed the first phase of their championship defense and pursuit of a repeat, but mindful of the ultimate goal they had for the season, they were clearly just getting started.

Chapter 2 – The Start of Something "Terribly" Good

In 1975 the Steelers had a radio color commentator by the name of Myron Cope. Those of us who grew up in western Pennsylvania during any portion of his three-plus decade stretch as the voice of the Steelers didn't just listen to him, we developed a relationship with him. We made him part of our families. We turned the television volume down and turned up the radio just to hear Steelers football his way, no, *our* way – the way we all came to know and love it and still reminisce about it today, because he was one of us.

Cope was a Pittsburgh native who initially cut his teeth in sports journalism through writing. His work appeared in Sports Illustrated, the Saturday Evening Post, and of course the hometown Post-Gazette. He was no slouch either, garnering national accolades aplenty for his ability to bring the drama and excitement of sports to live through the written word. But it was Cope's transition to the broadcast side that set the stage for his most enduring piece of work out of a career that saw him become a timeless figure in the story of the Pittsburgh Steelers.

The 1975 season was the first year that the NFL instituted a seeding system for the playoffs, breaking from the pre-determined rotating basis among divisions by which playoff matchups had been determined in years prior. The three division winning teams in each conference were seeded first through third in order of record, and the best second place finisher was awarded the Wild Card spot and fourth overall seed.

One caveat to the new format however was that two teams from the same division could not meet in the opening round of the playoffs. That rule came into play for the Steelers, as 11-3 Cincinnati would have been the fourth seed in the AFC by virtue of not winning a division title as opposed to the Baltimore Colts, who had a lesser record at 10-4 but did claim the championship of their division. As a result, Pittsburgh-Baltimore became the opening round matchup while Cincinnati traveled to Oakland to face the Raiders.

The opening round game set the stage for Cope's influence to come into play even more so than through his normal charge of firing up the radio audience with his signature "Yoi!" and "Double Yoi!" expressions. As the story goes, his boss at Pittsburgh's WTAE, the Steelers' flagship broadcast station at the time, told him to come up with a gimmick for fans to bring to the game that would help kick the crowd enthusiasm up an extra notch as the Steelers opened their Super Bowl defense.

Cope settled on towels; gold ones, to be exact. He reasoned that they were inexpensive, easily portable, lightweight, and – little did he know what was in store – a staple in nearly every home. He chose, as was one of his many clearly-evident talents, a catchy nickname to go along with the idea, and thus was born the Terrible Towel.

Cope's superiors at WTAE were somewhat unsure about his idea, but, he had done what they asked so they were inclined to optimistically run with it. Within the Pittsburgh locker room it was met with either indifference or dissent, many echoing Cope's original attitude of the Steelers not being the type of team that used, or needed, gimmicks to be successful. But Cope was the one whose job called for it, and so Terrible Towels would indeed be the item of the day in the Three Rivers stands.

What Cope, or the WTAE brass, or any of the players, or the tens of thousands of fans who were a part of the Towel's maiden voyage had no idea of was the magnitude and reach that it would develop. As we all cheer on our Steelers some 40-plus years later, we're accustomed to it being not just "a thing" but *the* thing that represents all of what we call Steeler Nation, which is really a misnomer as support for the Steelers extends quite literally to every corner of the globe.

The Terrible Towel has appeared at the top of Mt. Everest and at the Vatican. Steelers fans have taken it everywhere from the Sahara Desert to the Great Wall of China to the other Big Ben, the one in London. It's gone on combat patrols in Iraq and Afghanistan, tucked inside the body armor of service members with Pittsburgh ties to remind them of the pride and attitude that comes with being a Steelers fan.

It's been a prop at countless wedding receptions and it regularly swaddles newborn babies. For all that the Terrible Towel has become, Cope actually failed quite miserably at his charge. He didn't come up with a gimmick like WTAE asked him to, he gave life to the very item that unites and energizes Pittsburgh Steelers fans everywhere, and will continue to do so for as long as Sundays in the fall and winter are Steeler Sundays.

Terrible Towels and all, the Steelers' playoff defense of their Super Bowl title finally got underway at Three Rivers on December 27th, 1975. It was, not surprisingly, a typically frigid Pittsburgh day on the banks of the Allegheny River. The game-time temperature for the 1 PM kickoff was barely above freezing, and the accompanying wind chill gave a feel of barely more than 20 degrees. A light snow served as the final touch for the blustery winter day or, in other words, familiar Steelers playoff weather for the home crowd of just under 50,000.

The Colts earned their way into the playoffs by virtue of a head-to-head sweep of the Miami Dolphins, who they finished tied with atop the AFC East at 10-4. Baltimore notched a convincing 33-17 victory at Miami in the two teams' first meeting of the season in mid-November, then claimed a dramatic 10-7 overtime win against the Dolphins at home in the season's next-to-final week. In that hard-fought game that was every bit indicative of two clubs knowing they were likely setting the score for one remaining playoff spot as the other division leaders in the conference were pacing their way to 11- and 12-win records, the Colts fell behind 7-0 in the third quarter before tying the score in the fourth and then winning on a field goal in the extra period.

Beyond their success against the Dolphins, the Colts came into the postseason riding a nine game winning streak. After an abysmal 1-4 start they rebounded to defeat Joe Namath and the New York Jets on the road in the last week of October and never looked back, proceeding to run the table over the two months that followed. It was a turnaround of remarkable proportions for the Colts, who had finished the previous season tied for the worst record in the NFL at 2-12 and, as their start to the 1975 campaign indicated, didn't appear to be on pace to fare any better through the first third of the year.

Largely responsible for the Colts' dramatic improvement was first-year head coach Ted Marchibroda. Interestingly, Marchibroda was born and raised in Franklin, Pennsylvania, slightly over an hour north of Pittsburgh. The Steelers drafted him as a quarterback out of the University of Detroit in 1953, and he spent three seasons with Pittsburgh before finishing his playing career with the Chicago Cardinals in 1957 before getting into coaching. Marchibroda began his sideline career as a member of the Washington Redskins' staff and had stints with several NFL teams as he made his way through the coaching ranks before landing the top job in Baltimore.

Another interesting angle to the matchup was that it featured two Louisiana products at quarterback, the Steelers' Bradshaw and the Colts' Bert Jones. Baltimore drafted Jones out of Louisiana State University in 1973 with visions of him becoming the permanent replacement for Johnny Unitas. The Colts traded Unitas to San Diego following the 1972 season as his storied career had moved well into its twilight and his playing time had decreased over the preceding few years in favor of Marty Domres and Earl Morrall. Drafting Jones had all the makings of true fresh start for the Colts with a young and promising quarterback, and in 1975 Jones started all 14 regular season games for the first time in his brief career, playing a key role in the Colts' resurgence.

True to the adage that no quarterback can carry an offense on his own, Jones certainly had multiple weapons at his disposal. Wide receiver Glenn Doughty and running back Lydell Mitchell comprised much of the Baltimore offensive threat, and 1975 marked the first of three consecutive Pro Bowl seasons for Mitchell. How the multi-faceted Colts' attack would perform against the menacing challenge of the Steel Curtain was one of the chief storylines heading into the game, outside of the Steelers' newest item of fan paraphernalia, of course. Pittsburgh took to the Three Rivers turf for the Saturday matinee in their traditional home black jerseys over gold pants, while the visiting Colts appeared in all white from head to toe, with blue numbers and trim.

The Steelers faced a setback before the opening kickoff even took place though, as Greene was again unable to suit up due to the injury that had hampered him throughout most of the season's second half. The other members of the defense had indeed stepped up in his absence during that stretch, and the same "next man up" mentality would again be needed as the postseason commenced.

The game didn't exactly get off to a great start for the home squad. The Steelers fumbled the opening kickoff, setting up a golden opportunity for Baltimore to silence all of the golden towels being waved with an early score. Just a few plays into the possession though, Jones dropped back to pass but ultimately could not find an open target before the Steelers' defensive pressure got to him. Linebacker Jack Ham was the first to hit Jones with J.T. Thomas arriving a split second later. Thomas landed awkwardly on Jones' right arm, his throwing side, and the Colts' field general was unable to continue playing. In an instant, Baltimore's swift offensive attack had been significantly decimated. Domres came on in relief, a difficult assignment for sure having seen little playing time during the season and having to sort out his timing with the offense on the fly in a playoff contest at the home of the defending Super Bowl champions.

The Steelers did their best to give Domres a chance to succeed in the early going, continuing their less-than-stellar start. In addition to the botched opening kickoff Pittsburgh also committed a roughing the kicker penalty in the person of defensive tackle John Banaszak that allowed a would-be failed Colts' drive to continue, though the defense held firm and didn't allow Baltimore to score. The Steelers' defense bailing them out after mistakes was a prominent theme for the afternoon. Case in point was Ham continuing his impactful defensive play, intercepting Domres on a subsequent first quarter Baltimore possession.

Bradshaw and company quickly capitalized on Ham's takeaway, moving the ball into Baltimore territory and setting the stage for Harris to break the scoreless tie on a play from the Colts' 8-yard line. Harris took the handoff and swept left, getting a picture perfect block from pulling right guard Gerry Mullins to spring the initial running lane. He did the rest himself, dodging two Baltimore tacklers before barreling across the goal line for the first score of the afternoon. Roy Gerela converted the point after and the Steelers took a 7-0 lead, a mark that stood through the end of the first quarter. It was a short-lived lead though. On an ensuing Pittsburgh possession the hiccups that had marked the Steelers' performance in the initial fifteen minutes continued as the game entered the second quarter of play.

One particularly forgettable play came on a passing attempt that originated from just inside the Colts' end of the field. Dropping back near the Steelers' logo, Bradshaw sailed a pass to the right side of the field with no Steeler anywhere close to it. There were two Colts in the vicinity however, and one of them, defensive back Lloyd Mumphord, intercepted the ball and quickly turned up field with it. Colts' linebacker Tom MacLeod threw a timely block on Harris that sprung Mumphord to the outside of the field, where a host of Steelers players couldn't catch him as he walked a tightrope along the Pittsburgh sideline before finally being brought down near the Pittsburgh 20-yard line. While Mumphord certainly showed his skill in closing on the ball for the interception and making a dazzling return run, the play was yet another in the line of Pittsburgh mistakes that were keeping the Colts in the game.

Baltimore proceeded to even the score, as on the third down play that followed Domres took the snap and rolled out to his right, buying time behind solid pass protection from the Baltimore line before finding Doughty open in the back of the end zone. He delivered a strike, and just like that, or rather after kicker Toni Linhart delivered the extra point, the game was knotted at 7-7. The single-digit tie stood through the second quarter as the squads headed to their respective locker rooms for halftime.

The outcome up to that point had to be an encouraging result for the Colts on any day, but especially given the early setback they suffered with Jones' injury. On the flip side, it clearly wasn't the start to the game that the Steelers had sought. The contest was clearly showing characteristics of a game that was ripe for an unthinkable upset, one where the favorite allows the underdog to hang around just long enough through a series of errors and overall subpar play, then ultimately falls victim to a late barrage that they're unable to overcome with sheer talent.

As the third quarter commenced that storyline was perpetuated even further. On the Steelers' first offensive drive Harris fumbled deep inside Pittsburgh territory, giving the ball back to the Colts with an opportunity to forge ahead. And while they did indeed take the lead, thanks again to the staunch Pittsburgh defense it wasn't as detrimental of a surge as it could have been. The Steel Curtain clamped down and forced a field goal attempt, which Linhart converted from 21 yards away to give Baltimore a 10-7 advantage.

In championship fashion though, the Pittsburgh defense rose to the occasion for the remainder of the contest. On a day where the offense was clearly performing at a level less than its best, it took control of the football game and carried the Steelers. On a third down play later in the quarter, Domres delivered the ball to the left side of the field, a choice that quickly came to look like an extremely ill-advised one thanks to the speed with which the Steelers' defenders closed on the ball. Chief among them was Blount, who made the interception and proceeded to weave his way through traffic heading toward the Baltimore end zone, breaking a tackle attempt before finally being brought to the carpet near the Pittsburgh 7-yard line by Colts' guard Robert Pratt.

The Blount interception not only provided a much-welcomed jolt of enthusiasm throughout the stadium, not the least of which was desperately needed on the Pittsburgh sideline, but it also set the table perfectly for the Steelers' powerful running attack to take back the lead. That's exactly what happened, as Bleier took a handoff from Bradshaw and sidestepped his way through the maze of bodies to cover the remaining yardage, dragging Mumphord the final few steps as he crossed the goal line. Gerela was again successful on the point after, and the Steelers were back on top 14-10.

The bevy of golden towels waving throughout the stands were still a new and somewhat quizzical sight to everyone in Three Rivers, but with the Steelers finally seizing the lead they became exactly what the WTAE brass had hoped they would, a representation of the energy that was building and the enthusiasm that the home crowd had for their Steelers. That enthusiasm had continued opportunities to present itself as the game drew on, as after their slow start the Steelers were finally starting to resemble the team that had so dominantly plowed through the AFC that year.

After a failed Baltimore offensive possession, punter David Lee made matters even worse by shanking a kick out of bounds to set the Steelers' offense up with another round of prime field position. The punt was one of nine on the day for Lee, which in itself was an indicator of a team quelling its own chances for victory through an inability to generate offense.

That specific miscue however proved to be extra costly, and the ensuing Pittsburgh possession culminated in Bradshaw calling his own number to finish off the work with a two-yard touchdown run. Combined with Gerela's point after the quarterback keeper pushed the lead to 21-10 Pittsburgh as the fourth quarter got underway. With the Steelers finally coming alive and time also against them, the victory prospects that the Colts so optimistically held in the early stages of the game were beginning to rapidly erode.

But they weren't entirely gone. In a pull-out-all-the-stops move, Marchibroda summoned Jones back into the game, his early injury apparently manageable enough for him to attempt to valiantly salvage his team's season. Jones did have some success moving the Colts offense, which was perhaps energized by seeing their regular leader return in such a condition. Baltimore reached the Pittsburgh 3-yard line in the game's final minutes and appeared poised to notch the score that would bring them to within a fighting chance, though an onside kick and recovery would almost certainly be needed afterward to have any chance of scoring again.

Such strategy considerations quickly became a moot point however, as Jones took a snap from under center and faked a handoff then stood in the pocket surveying the end zone for an open receiver. As he held the ball, Ham managed to get around Colts' guard Elmer Collett and knock it out of Jones' hand. Linebacker Andy Russell was on the spot and picked up the fumble after it bounced directly upward from the turf. Russell began motoring down the right sideline, accompanied by a convoy of Steelers' blockers. Though not the fleetest of foot, Russell managed to traverse the entire 93-yard distance to cross the goal line and score the touchdown that cemented the Steelers' victory. Gerela's work afterward set the score at 28-10, which is how it remained as the clock ticked down to triple zeroes a few short moments later.

The Steelers had survived despite playing without the dominant Greene and delivering a performance that, by their standards, wasn't at all befitting of a team with their talent and aspirations. In reference to Cope's brainchild, the new golden towels, many could go as far as to have called the Steelers' performance "terrible" were it not for the way that the defense turned up the pressure in the second half to regain control of the game. A win was a win however, and the Steelers were safely on to the AFC Championship for the third time in four years.

Their opponent was determined just over 24 hours later, in an all too familiar setting. In the place where the Steelers had punched their ticket to their first-ever Super Bowl appearance just one day shy of a year prior, none other than their longtime nemesis the Oakland Raiders held off a late comeback attempt by the visiting Bengals to set up the much-anticipated and widely-predicted rematch between the two squads for AFC supremacy. The upcoming game offered two certainties –

that there would be a continuation of the bad blood that had defined the rivalry between the teams over the years, and that the Steelers would need to play much, much better than they had in their just-completed divisional round victory if they were to return to the Super Bowl.

Chapter 3 – Hardly a Warm Welcome

It took 15 games to get there, but in the end the 1975 season arrived at the place that deep down everyone figured it would. The Steelers and Raiders of course had no love lost between them, and throughout the regular season the idea that they were both simply jockeying for home field in the seemingly inevitable playoff matchup was a notion that few would doubt. The Steelers succeeded by finishing with one more victory, and after each club dispatched their first round opponents, the stage was set for the fourth consecutive postseason meeting between the two, a rematch of the previous year's penultimate tilt.

For the Steelers, returning to the Super Bowl would bring a chance to enter rarified air in the early years of the post-merger NFL by repeating as champions. For Oakland, aside from simply wanting to avenge their previous year's defeat after twelve months to think about it, was the motivation brought by the looming void of having so far failed to win a Super Bowl despite being one of the premier teams in football for several seasons.

The January weather was perfectly in line with the nature of the relationship between the two teams – bitter cold. While the Sunday matinee contest was held just days after the start of a brand new year, it was played amidst same old Pittsburgh winter. Conditions were such that during the week they undoubtedly caused many a local to grumble, but they quickly became an advantage when the weekend arrived and the warm weather Raiders had to make the cross-country trek to Three Rivers. The game time temperature hovered in the mid to upper teens while strong winds swirling about the stadium's concrete bowl structure made for an actual feel of single digits.

The Three Rivers artificial turf playing surface became as much of a storyline as the players that took to it for the game. The wintry weather rendered it frozen and slick, and despite the best efforts of the grounds crew to thaw it out in advance of kickoff, there was only so much that could be done in the battle against Mother Nature. The field conditions gave rise to the standard variety conspiracy theorists that seem to surface any time a warm weather team plays a critical game on the road against a cold weather opponent. This case was no different. There were some that suggested the Pittsburgh grounds crew was selective in its efforts to de-ice the field given that a slick track would pose more difficulty for the Raiders than it would for the well-acclimated Steelers, although it seemed far more likely that the conditions were simply equally bad for both sides.

In addition to the weather, the Steelers also had another advantage working in their favor, both practically and in an intangible sense, as Greene returned to the starting lineup. Seeing number 75 in uniform and ready to go was a welcome sight for everyone in the stadium, with the exception of those on the Oakland sideline of course. The Steelers, as always when playing at home, wore their black jerseys for the contest. The Raiders appeared somewhat less menacing in their road whites as opposed to their own black jerseys that they had worn the previous year when the teams met in Oakland. Ben Dreith served as the referee for the matchup. At the time the highlight of Dreith's career was having worked Super Bowl VIII in 1974, but little did anyone know he would go on to issue perhaps the most famous call in the history of football officiating, announcing that a Jets player was guilty of "giving him the business" when calling a 15-yard personal foul penalty in a 1986 game between New York and Buffalo.

The Steelers won the coin toss and elected to receive the opening kickoff. By the time local musician Al Homburg finished his rendition of the national anthem the Pittsburgh crowd was in a frenzy, the frigid temperatures for the moment not affecting their burning desire to see their Steelers take down their arch-nemeses. The Steelers placed the trio of running back Mike Collier, Blount, and defensive back Dave Brown between their own goal line and 10-yard line to receive the kickoff from Oakland's Ray Guy.

Guy's boot was a shorter one, and Collier fielded it near the Pittsburgh 15-yard line and dashed forward for about 15 return yards before being brought down by a host of Raiders led by running back and special teams player Jess Phillips. The opening play already brought a moment of excitement and a preview of what was in store for the afternoon as Collier lost control of the football upon being hit, prompting a brief scramble for it on the frozen turf. Blount emerged from the pile with possession, though Collier was ruled down by contact before the fumble.

Nonetheless it was a frantic start to the much-anticipated contest, one that was only perpetuated when on the first play from scrimmage the Raiders nearly jumped offside. Defensive end Otis Sistrunk anxiously jolted toward the line of scrimmage anticipating the snap but was able to pull back in time to avoid a penalty. On the second play of the drive Oakland's anticipation showed again. Linebacker Phil Villapiano barged through the Steelers' line to tackle Harris for a loss, showing early that the Raiders had come to play, cold weather or not.

Facing a third and fourteen situation after the first two running attempts went in reverse, Bradshaw took to the air for the first time on the afternoon and found tight end Larry Brown open on the far sideline right in front of the down marker. The officials spotted the ball inches short, and Noll elected to play things safely in the early going by bringing on punter Bobby Walden to try and pin the Raiders deep in their own zone. The Steelers downed Walden's kick near the Oakland 20-yard line after it fell to the turf, giving way to the defense for the first time on the frigid afternoon.

The Raiders wasted little time trying to establish the dynamic passing offense that nearly won them the AFC title matchup against Pittsburgh the year prior, despite the difficult conditions. On the second play of their opening drive quarterback Ken Stabler found tight end Bob Moore open across the middle of the field. It was a modest pickup, not enough to gain a first down, but it was a signal, similar to their early defensive vigor, that the Raiders intended to come out firing in their quest to take down the defending conference champions.

The next play served as an even stronger indicator. On third and short the Oakland line held its ground long enough to buy Stabler time, and the Raiders' quarterback responded by zipping a strike downfield to Mike Siani, a dangerous receiver who didn't play in the previous year's playoff matchup between the teams as his season was cut short by an injury. Siani's catch was good for not just a first down but also brought Oakland almost to midfield. The two early passes also showed that the icy field conditions were absolutely going to be a factor throughout the day for both sides. On the offensive half, Stabler faced a difficult time getting solid footing and had visibly lightened up his throw to Siani. In turn the Steelers' secondary players were having maneuverability troubles of their own, unable to quickly close on Siani as he ran his route and thus leaving him more open than would normally be the case on such a play.

The Raiders made their way into Pittsburgh territory on the heels of a few short running plays, one a carry from fullback Marv Hubbard, but stalled out shortly after crossing the midfield stripe. On the third and long play that they failed to convert, running back Clarence Davis was seemingly open on an out route to the near sideline but simply slipped on the turf, causing the ball to sail incomplete and bringing on Guy to punt the ball away. The Terrible Towels swirled wildly in the Three Rivers stands to acknowledge the home team's early defensive success, even if it was somewhat aided by good fortune.

Struggling to mount any kind of sustained attack given the conditions, the two sides traded possessions and reached the end of the first quarter tied 0-0. The Raiders did build some slight offensive momentum in the early moments of the second quarter, as aided by several Pittsburgh missteps they again moved the ball into Steelers territory. Facing a third and long situation, the Raiders were bailed out by a pass interference call against Steelers' safety Glen Edwards that brought them to just shy of midfield. Edwards vehemently disagreed with the call, getting in the face of the official and protesting demonstratively, but nonetheless the call stood. A few plays later Banaszak clipped off solid yardage on a run up the middle, and shortly after that the Steelers' defense committed another error by jumping offside, moving the ball to the Pittsburgh 30-yard line.

That was the extent of the Raiders' progress though, as like it had dome so many times throughout the year, the Steelers' defense rose to the occasion to stop the threat. On a third and six play that followed, Stabler dropped back to pass and fired a mid-range toss intended for tight end Moore near the far hash mark. The throw was slightly low, and Wagner dove in front of Moore to intercept it just inches before the ball hit the frozen turf.

Wagner immediately jumped to his feet and began returning the ball downfield, picking up additional yardage before being shoved out of bounds on the Oakland sideline just short of midfield. Being in enemy territory, if there really was such a thing for the Steelers in Three Rivers, didn't stop Wagner from mixing things up with the Raiders' Hubbard. The brief dust up drew a crowd but cooler heads ultimately prevailed.

Sensing the enormity of the opportunity at hand and knowing that chances were proving to be scarce on the day, Bradshaw wasted no time trying to capitalize. He opened the offensive series with a well-placed pass down the right sideline to Swann, who slipped free of two Oakland defenders to make the catch for a 20-yard gain. After Harris was stuffed for a loss on the following play, the tandem of Bradshaw and Swann tried to recreate their magic from moments earlier, running a very similar play that nearly produced similar results. Swann again found himself open, but at the last moment Raiders' safety Jack Tatum, always a factor in the rivalry, swooped in and delivered a rattling hit, knocking the ball loose from Swann's hands for an incompletion.

Harris gained another chunk of yardage on the following play, darting up the middle of the field for a nine yard gain but still falling short of a first down. The run did however bring Pittsburgh closer for kicker Roy Gerela, and given the conditions it was yardage that was certainly welcome. Gerela came on and drilled the 36-yard field goal attempt through the uprights to give Pittsburgh the first score and lead of the game at 3-0. It was a wise coaching move by Noll and a clutch moment of execution by Gerela that would loom large in the later stages of the contest.

Gerela's kick proved to be the only points not just of the first half but of the first three quarters, showing that the game was absolutely a contest between three opponents, the Steelers and Raiders as well as the weather. Both teams looked like a shell of the championship caliber clubs that they truly were as a result of the conditions limiting them in their playmaking abilities. On one particularly frustrating sequence late in the third quarter the two sides traded turnover after turnover in succession. The Raiders were in the midst of their most productive possession of the afternoon, reaching the Pittsburgh 11-yard line with visions of finally cracking the end zone, when running back Pete Banaszak caught a pass in the left flat and fumbled without so much as being touched by a Steeler, the icy glaze on the ball simply rendering it impossible to maintain control of. Lambert recovered, but the Steelers' possession was short lived.

On the Steelers' first play after taking over possession Bradshaw came up throwing, finding Swann open over the middle of the field near the logo on the 50-yard line. Swann caught the pass in mid-stride, but immediately upon turning up field was met with a vicious arm swipe from Raiders' safety George Atkinson.

The hit not only jarred the ball loose but also brought Swann to the turf. Tatum recovered the fumble near the left hash mark area of the field. To make matters worse, Swann had to be helped from the field and ultimately taken to the locker room and on to a local hospital as a result of Atkinson's hit, with early reports from the team medical staff indicating that he had suffered a concussion on the play. In addition to the long-term concern for his health, Swann's loss clearly hampered the Steelers' offensive attack by stripping Bradshaw of one of his top targets for the remainder of the game.

Stabler went to work as the Raiders' offense returned, again finding his favorite target on the day, Siani, open along the sideline for a completion that brought Oakland to the Steelers' 35-yard line with just over two minutes remaining in the third quarter. Davis moved the ball further on the next play, gaining five yards the hard way by going straight up the middle. Stabler went right back to Davis on the next play, but he didn't enjoy the same success. Sweeping to his right, Davis was met by the Steelers' Thomas who made a textbook hit by lowering his shoulder to jar the ball loose. Lambert recovered and the offensive pendulum swung back in favor of the Pittsburgh.

On second down and nine the Steelers found some success from the passing game. John Stallworth made a diving grab of, and held on to, no small feat given the troubles both sides were having in that regard, a Bradshaw pass that netted Pittsburgh ten yards. The Steelers were further aided by a personal foul call against the Raiders, as Villapiano delivered a late hit after Stallworth was already down by contact. The penalty moved the Steelers just inside of Oakland territory where after one more play, a minimal gain by Harris, the whistle blew signifying the end of the third quarter. With fifteen minutes to go the Steelers held a contentious 3-0 lead in their attempt to retain the AFC title.

The final fifteen minutes held in store an outburst by both sides that nobody saw coming on the icy Pittsburgh day though, one that would propel one team onward to the Super Bowl and for the other amount to too little too late.

Chapter 4 – Saving the Best for Last

Championships are beautiful, magnificent, and timelessly preserved. Their good qualities are remembered for eternity, their highlights played over and over on both actual reels as well as the figurative ones that exist in the minds of everyone that witnessed them being won. Championships are the beautiful exterior, the freshly-polished coating. They're marked by shiny rings and trophies and banners, recognized with parades and parties and celebrations. But underneath, they're not always pretty. Far from it. Winning a championship often times takes, even more so than skill or execution or properly-channeled aggression, a resolve to withstand ugly stretches, to persevere through challenges and not always get it done the glamorous way, but get it done nonetheless.

Entering the fourth quarter against Oakland with the AFC championship on the line, the Steelers found themselves in exactly such a scenario. The first three quarters had been a stalemate with the lone exception of Gerela's kick, as the weather the clear winner over both teams. Just moving was a challenge, let alone toting an icy football against a ruthless opponent, yet it was no secret that sooner or later one side was going to crack the proverbial code. Whichever side was going to become AFC champions would have to earn their ticket to Miami, where Super Bowl X was scheduled to be played in two weeks, the hard way.

Like two heavyweight fighters in a title bout, the Steelers and Raiders pulled out all of the stops in that final quarter, caring not for appearance but focusing only on getting a result. Similar to a frantic flurry of punches in the final seconds of a boxing round that are in contrast to the more measured pace of the opening minutes, the teams let loose for the game's final stanza, knowing that each of their seasons were on the line and, quite frankly, so too were significant aspects of their legacies. From the very first snap, the fourth quarter delivered what the game had lacked leading up to it – back and forth, battle-it-out football between two bitter rivals and talented teams.

The quarter began with a welcome sight for the Steelers in the person of number 32. Kept under wraps most of the day by a strong Oakland run defense, Harris swung outside and caught a short Bradshaw pass, then proceeded to gain several additional yards, meeting the host of Raiders tacklers head on and driving forward for more before being brought down at the Raiders' 25-yard line. Harris showed an extra dose of tenacity on the run, almost as if he simply had enough after being held in check for so long, and was determined to break out when his team most needed it.

On the next play he further confirmed that to be the case.

The Steelers stuck with the hot hand, and Harris took Bradshaw's handoff and bounced to the left side of the field. What happened next was a treat to watch, a display of both power and speed that once again proved great players can't be stopped so much as they can only be contained for a while. Oakland defensive back Neal Colzie was the first Raider to meet Harris, standing him up near the line of scrimmage for what would have been no gain. But there was simply no stopping Harris on the play. He shrugged off Colzie with sheer strength then outran the next pursuer, linebacker Ted Hendricks, as he darted down the sideline and into the end zone. Gerela's extra point made the score 10-0 Steelers, and the Three Rivers crowd came fully alive over the prospect of a 10-point lead with less than a quarter to go on a day where just moving the ball for any amount of time had proven difficult.

The Raiders got a strong return from Banaszak on the ensuing kickoff though and began their next drive from their own 40-yard line. After an incomplete pass attempt to Siani on the opening play, one that drew the ire of both Siani and Raiders' coach John Madden for what they thought should have been a pass interference call, Stabler connected with tight end Dave Casper in the middle of the field for a 23-yard gain that again brought the Raiders into Steelers' territory. Oakland stuck with what worked on the following play, again harnessing the Stabler-to-Casper connection to advance further into Steelers' territory. Casper made a strong grab among double coverage on the play, hauling in the pass despite being sandwiched by Lambert and Wagner.

The "fool me twice, shame on me" adage became all too appropriate on the next play, as Stabler connected with Casper for a third consecutive completion. This one was of the crossing variety, as Casper zipped horizontally over the middle of the field and grabbed the ball before being forced out of bounds on the near sideline at the Steelers' 14-yard line. Casper becoming the immediate threat drew attention away from Stabler's other key target on the day, Siani, which came to bear on the following play. Benefitting from great protection by his line, Stabler stood in the pocket and waited for Siani to work his way open on a slant route to the middle of the end zone, then delivered the ball perfectly for Siani to haul in for the touchdown. Blanda did his part afterward and the Steelers lead that just moments earlier looked quite comfortable was again reduced to a slim one at 10-7.

The much-anticipated title matchup now seemed to be frantically trying to make up for its extended slow start, as more action had taken place in the first five minutes of the fourth quarter than through the entire first 45 minutes. That trend continued on the following kickoff, as the Steelers' Collier fielded Guy's kick and darted up the left sideline, slashing through would-be Oakland tacklers as he quickly crossed the midfield stripe. Guy managed to get just enough of a hit on Collier to bring him down near the Raiders' 40-yard line and save what otherwise would have been a sure touchdown, as Collier was visibly agitated at having been stopped by the kicker when he came to his feet after the play ended.

The Steelers didn't capitalize on Collier's magnificent runback though, failing to move the chains on the next series and ending up in a punt situation. They were fortunate that their fate wasn't worse, as on third down disaster nearly struck in the form of an interception. Bradshaw dropped back and fired a pass over the middle that sailed into a triangle of Raiders' defenders. It hit defensive back Charlie Philips in the hands but the rookie couldn't hold on, forcing a fourth down and bringing on Walden to try and pin the Raiders deep in their own zone. Walden's kick was short, fielded by Siani near the Oakland 20-yard line, but the Steelers' coverage team quickly got downfield to make the stop and limit him to all but no return.

A sense of nervousness moved over the Three Rivers crowd as the change in possession represented a critical juncture of the game. Oakland had built some momentum on their previous offensive possession, mounting a quick strike scoring drive in under two minutes largely by way of their potent aerial attack that had finally come alive. With the Steelers stalling out on their most recent offensive series the

Raiders appeared poised to take control of the game with another score as Stabler led his charges on to the field.

The Raiders began with a run, perhaps to set up another passing play later in the sequence, but would have no such opportunity. Stabler handed off to Hubbard who was quickly met at the line of scrimmage by Greenwood. The ball popped loose and rolled forward for a moment before none other than Lambert fell on it, recovering for the Steelers at the Oakland 25-yard line. It was the tenth combined turnover between the two teams on the afternoon, and Lambert's third fumble recovery. It was also a catalyst that got the home crowd re-ignited, imploring their Steelers to again distance themselves from the Raiders, this time for good.

Bradshaw saw to it that they didn't let their faithful followers down. After two short Harris runs netted a combined five yards, the Steelers called a passing play on third down. Bradshaw took the snap and surveyed the scene downfield, finding Stallworth in the front left corner of the end zone and letting the ball fly in his direction. It was a gamble on Bradshaw's part for sure as two Oakland defenders were within arm's reach of Stallworth. But in a combination of skill and some more luck, or rather simply the Steelers' latest turn at being on the good side of the weather's ruthless impact on the game, one of the Raiders in the vicinity, Colzie, slipped on the slick carpet while Stallworth elevated and made the catch for a touchdown to put the Steelers back in the lead, 16-10.

The Steelers paid their dues to the weather on the point after though, although in a far less detrimental fashion than the blow the Raiders had just absorbed. Walden wasn't able to handle the snap cleanly, leaving Gerela to pick up the ball and briefly scramble before attempting what could only barely and in the loosest sense be classified as a drop kick for the extra point, as the ball barely traveled a few feet before falling to the turf. Despite the botched play the Steelers were back in the driver's seat on the road to the Super Bowl, and with the game's end drawing closer their fans were absolutely letting the Raiders know it.

But as a true championship battle goes, the game was far from over.

In fact, there was almost an entire game's worth of action in the final ten minutes, or at least it felt that way for the frantic Steelers fans holding their breath as if to will the clock to reach triple zeroes with the lead intact. With the Steelers needing only to protect the ball and drain the clock as much as they could on their next offensive possession, Bleier fumbled. The Raiders were unable to capitalize, punting back to Pittsburgh, but would get yet another chance to claw their way back into the game as the clock ticked down past two minutes remaining.

First Bradshaw was felled, visibly shaken up after taking a sharp hit from Raiders' linebacker Monte Johnson as he tried to get to the ground to avoid such a tackle on a running play.

Backup Terry Hanratty came on as Bradshaw left the field accompanied by team staffers and being cheered loudly by the appreciative Pittsburgh fans, but on the very next play Harris committed the twelfth combined turnover of the afternoon, an almost unfathomable total for a conference championship game, by fumbling at the Raiders' 35-yard line with a minute and a half remaining. Hendricks darted into the line and, in a slightly different fashion than so many of the other fumbles by both sides where initial contact was enough to jar the overly slippery ball loose, had to wrestle it from Harris' hands amidst the pile up.

The Raiders had one final breath of life left. Ninety seconds to not only score a touchdown but also successfully negotiate an onside kick and get into reasonable field goal range for Blanda. It was a daunting task for sure, but on a day that had already seen more than its share of oddities and in the most classic of rivalry scenarios, clearly anything was possible. Stabler got right to business and in an ironic twist that fit right in with the crazy nature of the game, completed a long downfield pass to another of his prolific aerial attack weapons, this time one that had been entirely nonexistent on the afternoon but made a huge play for the Raiders in the prior year's AFC title game, Cliff Branch. Branch's first catch of the day was brave in addition to being timely. He lost his helmet when he was met by a Blount and Lambert sandwich but held on to the ball, giving Oakland a first down just inside Pittsburgh territory.

On the next play Stabler again looked for Branch, finding him on an out route to the left sideline. The pass was a bit high, and coupled with Blount's airtight coverage, resulted in an incompletion that stopped the clock with exactly one minute standing between the Steelers and a return to the Super Bowl. One minute separating the frenzied, Terrible Towel-waving Three Rivers crowd from seeing their Steelers punch their ticket to the biggest event in sports right before their very eyes. And, of course, one more minute for the Steel Curtain defense to hold strong and prove yet again that it was the best in the game by shutting down the Raiders in an absolute moment of truth.

The Steelers quickly found that winning that one minute would come by bending but not breaking. On the following play Stabler again zipped the ball down the middle of the field, reprising his target of choice from the earlier scoring drive in Casper. The Raiders' tight end hauled in the pass near the Pittsburgh 35-yard line with 45 seconds remaining, but got no more yardage, as Lambert again was the man on the spot for Pittsburgh, wrestling Casper to the turf. With the game clock ticking down toward 30 seconds remaining, Stabler hit Siani on a crossing pattern on the next play, but he was quickly brought down inside the field of play by Lambert once again, with help from fellow linebacker Marv Kellum. As a result, the Raiders were forced to use their final timeout to stop the clock with 24 seconds remaining in the game.

The tension inside Three Rivers Stadium had reached a palpable level as Oakland emerged from the sideline huddle and the two squads again lined up across from each other. In a twist of irony that fit perfectly with the theme of the afternoon, Stabler's next passing attempt was a deep ball to the right side of the end zone intended for Bradshaw – Morris Bradshaw, the Raiders' second year receiver whose season reception total was only in the single digits but whose speed made him an ideal weapon for the type of situation the Raiders were in. It fell incomplete as Bradshaw couldn't stay in bounds and get a hand on the ball, leaving Oakland with 17 seconds left to try and close the scoreboard gap.

In a surprise yet well-reasoned move, Madden then opted to bring in Blanda on third down to attempt a 41-yard field goal instead of running another play in order to save precious seconds on the clock. Blanda made good on his end, drawing Oakland closer at 16-10 and setting up an onside kick attempt with 12 seconds to go. If the Raiders were to recover they'd have one or two attempts downfield to score the tying touchdown, while if the Steelers recovered they could officially pack their bags for Miami. Though onside kicks are typically a long shot, on a day when slippery field conditions and near-frostbitten hands prevailed it was a true case of no outcome being impossible.

And, surely enough, the near impossible didn't just become possible, it became reality.

Guy skipped the ball to the left side of the field, where the first Steeler to touch it was receiver Reggie Garrett. The ball bounced off of Garrett's hands though and into the oncoming pile of traffic from both sides, a scrum that again resembled the fight for the football in the previous year's championship matchup at nearly the same spot on the field nonetheless, when Bradshaw had inexplicably fumbled late in the game. After the scuffle had settled down and the officials could peel players away from the pile the signal was clear, much to the dismay of the pins-and-needles crowd. It was Oakland's football, as Hubbard ultimately secured the loose ball. The Raiders, with seven seconds to go, had one final gasp of hope.

With no timeouts remaining Stabler lofted a pass downfield and toward the sideline, and again to the dismay of the crowd, Branch elevated above the Steelers' defenders to make the catch near the Pittsburgh 15-yard line. Trying desperately to get to the white line just feet away to stop the clock and give his team one more chance to get in the end zone though proved to be a fruitless endeavor for Branch. Blount quickly wrapped both arms around him, bringing him to the turf in bounds and enabling the clock to continue running until it expired, bringing victory for the Steelers. The Pittsburgh fans stormed the field, celebrating their team's second consecutive American Football Conference championship and Super

Bowl berth with an extra flair after having beaten the much-despised Raiders in the process.

The scene at Three Rivers was sheer pandemonium as fans continued to engulf the players from both sides as they tried to quickly reach the safety of their respective locker rooms. For the Raiders, it would be a somber locker room indeed. Yet another crushing defeat at the hands of their bitter rivals. Down the hallway in the bowels of Three Rivers, the Pittsburgh locker room was in the throes of a celebration. The Steelers had managed to fight their way to victory, to stave off the elements and their own mistakes and a last ditch attempt by a hungry opponent to again reach the season's final game and with it, have the opportunity to join an elite club within the National Football League as back-to-back Super Bowl champions.

Just moments later across the country in Los Angeles, the Rams and Dallas Cowboys kicked off the NFC Championship Game, playing for the right to be the Steelers' opponent in Super Bowl X. While for the moment the Steelers could breathe a sigh of relief and enjoy their victory, there was no doubt plenty of attention being paid to the locker room televisions and radio broadcasts to see who they'd face in Miami two weeks later. In the evening hours on the east coast, the Steelers got their answer. Dallas entered the L.A. Coliseum and dominated the Rams from the opening kickoff, never trailing on their way to a 37-7 victory and setting the stage for a Steelers-Cowboys Super Bowl.

Chapter 5 – Champions Don't Panic

Super Bowl X was played against a backdrop strikingly different from the previous year's contest in New Orleans. While the 1975 game featured a cold, slick field and overcast afternoon, the 1976 game in Miami's Orange Bowl came under sunny south Florida skies. It was also different in that both teams were vying for their second title and a place among the NFL's true elite franchises of the early post-merger era. Dallas had been to the big game twice already, losing Super Bowl V to the Colts in the very same Orange Bowl venue before defeating Miami the following year in Super Bowl VI.

Despite those successes, the 1975 Dallas squad's Super Bowl appearance was a bit of a surprise. Many believed at the start of the season and even the playoffs that there were much stronger NFC contenders. But on the heels of a magnificent play, the Cowboys upset the Vikings in Minnesota in the divisional playoff round when quarterback Roger Staubach heaved a 50-yard touchdown pass in the final minute of the game. The inspiring victory may very well have given the Cowboys extra momentum going up against the Rams the following week, as they again defeated a higher-seeded and seemingly superior team on the road. So while many questioned the Cowboys' viability against the Steelers, they entered the game loose and ready to continue playing as if they had nothing to lose, a strategy that had worked just fine for them up to that point in the post season.

For the Steelers it was very clear what was at stake. The chance to become a repeat champion and firmly cement themselves as one of the NFL's early dynasties awaited. But leading up to the contest they faced the very real prospect that to do so they'd have to earn a victory without Swann, one of their most prolific offensive threats, as he was still recovering from the vicious hit and resultant concussion he sustained at the hands of Atkinson in the AFC championship. While many on both the medical and football sides of the matter said Swann seemed like a long shot to suit up and Cowboys' safety Cliff Harris even made an attempt at gamesmanship in the media by suggesting that if Swann did play he'd certainly be thinking about the possibility of getting hit hard again, Swann was remarkably in the lineup when kickoff time finally arrived.

While Staubach, a Naval Academy graduate who served in Vietnam prior to pursuing his professional football career, was the team's on-field leader, coach Tom Landry was the overall boss. Landry was in his 16th season at the helm of the Cowboys and had led them to playoff appearances in eight of the previous nine years. Landry was known for his sideline apparel that consisted of a suit and his signature fedora hat, overly formal dress in an era when nearly all coaches had moved to the more casual look of team apparel such as polo shirts and pullover sweaters or jackets. Fashion wasn't the real area where Landry stood out though. He was widely-regarded as one of the game's great minds, the creator of both the 4-3 and "flex" defenses and an early pioneer of using data and analysis of opponents' tendencies to help inform game planning efforts.

Reversing their attire from the previous year's Super Bowl, the Steelers wore their black jerseys as it was the AFC's turn to be the home team, while the Cowboys as the visitors from the NFC donned their white jerseys with blue trim and silver pants and helmets. The referee for the game was Norm Schachter, who had worked the inaugural Super Bowl as well as the Dallas loss in Super Bowl V and also had the distinction of officiating the first-ever Monday Night Football contest. The Cowboys won the coin toss and elected to receive the opening kick, moving right to left cross the field as television viewers saw the game.

After the pregame pomp and circumstance had ended and the time to play football arrived, running backs Preston Pearson and Doug Dennison stood deep to receive the kick for Dallas. Gerela booted the ball into the air and Super Bowl X was officially underway. Pearson fielded the ball near the Dallas 5-yard line on the left side of the field but quickly broke toward his right. Swooping across from the opposite side of the field was another Dallas player who would become one of the most famous figures in Steelers-Cowboys Super Bowl lore in the future but for the moment was simply the co-contributor to the Cowboys' opening act.

Thomas "Hollywood" Henderson, a speedy linebacker, took the reverse from Pearson and darted up the left sideline, eating up yardage as he crossed into Steelers' territory before Gerela made a diving tackle to force him out of bounds and save a touchdown. The play certainly wasn't the start the Steelers were seeking, while for the Cowboys it was a tremendous momentum boost to catch the Steelers with a dose of trickery right out of the gate.

Staubach led the Dallas offense on to the field for the first time, and was immediately met with resistance in the form of L.C. Greenwood. Greenwood, who in the previous year's Super Bowl had delivered the hit on Minnesota quarterback Fran Tarkenton that led to a Steelers' safety midway through the second quarter, became an immediate factor in this Super Bowl game. He broke through the Dallas line and stripped the ball from Staubach, establishing the Steelers' defensive presence early even though Cowboys' center John Fitzgerald recovered to retain possession. The Cowboys couldn't produce any offense for the remainder of the possession and were forced to punt, giving Bradshaw and the Pittsburgh offense their first opportunity to shine in the bright Florida sun.

The rushing attack of Harris and Bleier was critical to the Steelers' success in their Super Bowl IX victory the year prior, and Pittsburgh clearly demonstrated an effort to again establish their dominance on the ground in the early going. The tandem ate up yardage by the chunks, bringing the Steelers to near midfield before they faced a third and one situation where Harris was brought down behind the line of scrimmage for a loss, forcing Pittsburgh into its own punt situation just as Dallas had been after its first series. Walden came on and, in a simple mental error, bobbled the snap, dropping it in front of himself. He caught the ball on the rebound but was quickly swarmed by a host of Cowboys and brought down for the second major momentum boost in the game's opening minutes.

In the immediate aftermath of Walden's mistake however, there was a subtle reason to remain calm even in the face of such an unfortunate error early in the game. Greene came over to Walden after the play and simply put his arm around the punter's head, clearly saying something to him. Given Greene's unquestioned team leadership it could be ascertained that it was a brief bit of encouragement, realizing the significant role Walden played in the Steelers' last Super Bowl victory when the game was at many times a battle of field position and knowing they could very well need him to be just as impactful as the current one played out.

Staubach sensed the opportunity at hand and went for the strike immediately when Dallas took over on offense. He spotted Pearson darting across the field from the far side to near and completed a pass to him in the center of the field that enabled the speedy receiver to turn up field along the sideline and outrun Russell on the way to the end zone for the first score of the game. Kicker Toni Fritsch converted the extra point to give Dallas an early 7-0 lead.

The previous season the Steelers won the Super Bowl largely thanks to answering the call when they needed to. They atoned for every mistake they made, picked each other up after every blunder, and ultimately had an answer for everything the Vikings threw at them. They showed the same resolve in the face of the opening Dallas score, as Bradshaw calmly brought the offense back on to the field and went straight to work after Blount returned the ensuing kickoff to the 33-yard line. Again sticking with a healthy dose of Harris and Bleier, the Pittsburgh offense marched up the Orange Bowl field unfazed by the Cowboys' early success.

The first four plays of the series saw Harris and Bleier alternate duty toting the football, each biting off moderate chunks of yardage to move the chains and move the Steelers to the just inside Dallas territory at the 48-yard line. The drive was moving well, although the Steelers were doing little to make their choice of plays difficult for the Cowboys to deduce. But, if anyone really knew those Steelers, they realized that simply riding their two workhorse backs wasn't their only strategy.

On second and five Bradshaw broke the trend of running plays and dropped back, looking downfield and launching a long spiral for Swann who made a leaping catch over Cowboys' cornerback Mark Washington. Swann landed gracefully along the sideline to keep his feet in bounds and put the Steelers at the Dallas 16-yard line. From there the Steelers resumed their regularly-scheduled programming on offense, with Harris and Bleier each carrying once again.

On third and one from the Dallas seven though, the Steelers threw the Cowboys for a loop with their next play call. With the running game consistently producing four and five yard gains, it seemed entirely likely that a short-yardage situation inside the 10-yard line would be cause for a similar run. Assuming success in getting at least the one needed yard, it would set up a first and goal and Pittsburgh would have four chances to crack the end zone from mere yards away. Dallas loaded up at the line of scrimmage in anticipation, which was all that the savvy veteran Bradshaw needed to see in order to exploit the weakness it left in the defensive backfield. He took the snap and rolled quickly to his right, tossing a short pass to wide open tight end Randy Grossman who waltzed untouched into the end zone to tack the Steelers' first six points on the board. Gerela's kick moments later made the score 7-7, and after the shaky start the Steelers were right back even with Dallas in a brand new game.

The way the afternoon proceeded from that point, it was as if there was indeed a brand new game that didn't begin until hours later as both teams' offensive production ground to a near halt. Dallas put together a sustained drive on its following possession, traveling 55 yards over the course of 10 minutes as the first quarter ended and the second began, but stalled out at the Steelers' 19-yard line and had to settle for a Fritsch field goal that moved the score to 10-7. While that score may have been nothing overly noteworthy, in the moments that followed though the Steelers, one in particular, would turn in one of the most memorable plays in Super Bowl, and all of football, history.

Starting their offensive possession from deep in their own territory after a Mitch Hoopes punt pinned them at their own 6-yard line, the Steelers reeled off two running plays that netted a combined four yards and put them in a third and long situation. An obvious passing opportunity, Bradshaw dropped back on the next play and aired out a high spiral toward the middle of the field for Swann. He was covered closely by Washington again, and when the two players both leapt for the ball, their hands each got a piece of it at the same time, causing it to pop directly up in the air as they both fell to the turf.

In an amazing display of concentration and body control, the image of which has since become emblazoned on framed photos and magazine covers and played over and over on highlight shows as it rightfully should be, Swann kept his eyes fixed on the ball as he fell downward and hauled it in for a 53-yard reception. As if that effort wasn't enough, Swann also had the presence of mind to get up and continue running, believing, correctly, that he was not yet down because Washington hadn't touched him after establishing possession. He barreled forward to the Dallas 37-yard line before finally being tackled, for good this time, by Cowboys' cornerback Mel Renfro.

The play wasn't, however, enough by itself to ignite a touchdown drive. The Steelers manufactured some more yardage but couldn't get beyond the Cowboys' 19-yard line, where they called on Gerela for a 36-yard field goal attempt with less than 30 seconds remaining until halftime. Dallas tried the age-old strategy of "icing the kicker" and called a timeout to give Gerela just a bit longer to contemplate his approach. Whether or not that directly impacted the attempt remains unknown, but regardless of the cause, Gerela pushed the kick wide left, leaving the score at 10-7 Dallas as the game reached intermission.

As the Steelers headed to the locker room they could be pleased that they were only trailing by a field goal given the multiple mistakes they had made, but at the same time they undoubtedly had to be mindful of the potential points they left on the table as well as those they allowed Dallas to put on the board, as a result. To distill the entire season down to 30 minutes of football for the world championship though, and with the personnel they had on both sides of the ball, they ultimately had to be happy with the position they were in.

Indeed, the remainder of the afternoon hinged on execution. Being able to deliver in the clutch, to make the offensive plays to put points on the board in quantities of six and to stand firm on defense and not allow the Cowboys to do the same. In other words, they needed two quarters of Pittsburgh Steelers football to bring home a second Super Bowl victory, two quarters of championship caliber play to stake their claim to a special piece of football history.

Chapter 6 – What Really Mattered

The 10-7 tally remained through the third quarter as neither team scored and, despite it being clearly obvious what was at stake, both tried their best to aid the other in taking the lead. Staubach tossed an interception early in the quarter, and Gerela missed another field goal attempt. In all, the two players that seemed to get the most action were the punters, as Walden and Hoopes were both called into action multiple times after stalled offensive drives. The fourth quarter began on a Hoopes punt as the Cowboys couldn't convert yet another a third down play, and after he delivered his kick the Steelers nearly made another costly mistake.

Brown and Edwards were back to receive for the Steelers. Brown fielded the ball just shy of the Pittsburgh 20-yard line, but fumbled after being immediately hit by a contingent of Cowboys. A scramble ensued on the Orange Bowl carpet, but in the end Thomas secured the football to retain possession for Pittsburgh. In a wild turn of events, after avoiding near disaster the Steelers nearly retook the lead on the very next play. Bradshaw dropped back and, unable to find a receiving target open, bought some time thanks to stellar protection by his offensive line. He rolled to his right and then dropped a medium range pass to Harris along the sideline, in the pocket between levels of the Cowboys' defense. Harris turned up field with a burst of speed and appeared to be off to the races, nothing between him and the end zone expect wide open turf, and the closest Cowboy to the play having fallen down trying to defend the pass.

But it wasn't to be. The officials blew the play dead, ruling that Harris had stepped out of bounds at the Steelers 43-yard line, his foot just barely grazing the white paint of the sideline and negating the beautiful catch and run. The Steelers tried to capture the missed yardage on the next play, as Bradshaw looked down the middle of the field for a streaking Stallworth but couldn't connect, overthrowing him by a step after he had broken free of the Cowboys' defenders Renfro and Harris. Though they had yet to strike pay dirt, it was clear the Steelers were approaching the game's final quarter aggressively, the experience of trailing in the Super Bowl foreign to them compared to how the previous year's game has progressed.

But quick changes of fate are all too common in playoff football, and after literally being a toe and a set of fingertips away from charging back into the lead on each of the previous two plays, the Steelers then saw their fortunes go in exactly the opposite direction. Harris was wrapped up for a four-yard loss by a swarming gang of Dallas defenders led by tackle Jethro Pugh. On the ensuing third-and-twelve situation from the Pittsburgh 41-yard line, things went from bad to worse. Bradshaw dropped back to pass but Dallas tackle Randy White found his way through the offensive line, causing the Steelers' quarterback to have to duck and scramble, both of which were to no avail. White corralled Bradshaw near the sideline with an assist from tackle Bill Gregory for a loss of 14 yards that brought the ball all the way back at the Pittsburgh 27-yard line, bringing Walden and the punt team on to the field.

It was then that Greene's unmistakable leadership in picking his punter back up after Walden's early mistake appeared to pay dividends. With the clock ticking away and on the heels of an offensive drive that quickly went in reverse, the Steelers needed Walden to deliver in a clutch moment, to essentially be an extension of the defense by using his leg to drive Dallas back in their own zone and not allow them to start the next possession with a short field. He did exactly that, to about as fine of a degree as any punter could. Walden got off a high, booming kick that sent the Cowboys' return man, receiver Golden Richards, backpedaling nearly 10 yards before finally catching the ball near the Dallas 15-yard line. The monster punt allowed plenty of time for the Pittsburgh coverage team to get downfield and into position so that Richards got little in the way of return yardage, as they forced him out of bounds at the Dallas 19-yard line.

Walden's success appeared to inspire the Steelers' defense on the next series, as it came out in dominant fashion and heartened the Pittsburgh faithful's hopes that a comeback, and a Super Bowl repeat, was still very much within reach. The Cowboys tried a dose of trickery on the first play as Staubach handed off to Pearson who immediately pitched the ball back to his quarterback for a pass attempt. The only problem was that the Steel Curtain had the Dallas receiving corps blanketed in coverage, forcing Staubach to try to run the ball. He didn't get far, as Steelers' tackle Steve Furness was waiting to make the stop for a one yard loss. Furness reprised the same role on the following play, jamming the line and stuffing a rushing attempt by Dennison as teammates Wagner and Ham combined to finish off the stop.

The Steelers tormented Dallas even more on the next play, as Staubach, operating from the shotgun, again struggled to find an open receiver and couldn't outmaneuver the swarming mass of black and gold. Furness, White and Greenwood combined for the sack, dropping the Cowboys' quarterback for a three yard loss and setting up a brilliant opportunity as the Cowboys were forced to punt from their own 16-yard line. It stood to reason that Pittsburgh would get favorable field position unless Hoopes could replicate Walden's enormous kick from the previous series, but the Steelers' defense had an even better idea.

A better idea like tacking two points on the board before the offense got its turn with the ball again. For the second straight year the Steelers notched a safety in the Super Bowl, this one coming as Reggie Harrison burst through the middle of the Dallas protection to block Hoopes' kick. It rolled out of the back of the end zone, cutting the deficit to one point at 10-9 Dallas and prompting a free kick from the Cowboys. More than just two points though, the play brought an obvious shift in the game's momentum. While still trailing, the Steelers had moved into position to take control, and given their earlier close calls on offense it seemed as if the time was right for Bradshaw and company to assert themselves on the upcoming possession.

Collier fielded the free kick near the Pittsburgh 30-yard line. He had a strong blocking contingent in front of him in Edwards and rookie defensive back Dave Brown, enabling him to cross into Dallas territory before being brought down at the 45-yard line. The Steelers' play selections as they began their latest offensive march came as little surprise. Harris and Bleier shouldered the load again, each carrying twice to move the ball to the Dallas 28-yard line.

But on second and nine after scrambling for what seemed like a healthy gain, Bradshaw fumbled the ball along the near sideline. The hearts of everyone in black and gold skipped a beat momentarily, and a collective sigh of relief quickly came over Pittsburgh fans as the ball bounced out of bounds, keeping possession with the Steelers. After narrowly averting disaster on a drive that began as a promising opportunity, the Steelers couldn't convert the third and one play when Bradshaw and Harris briefly collided with each other on the exchange and Harris was stopped short of the line to gain by roughly a foot. The result brought about a decision for Noll, who opted to bring on Gerela for the field goal attempt instead of going for the short fourth down conversion despite Gerela's struggles on the day. Gerela didn't make it stress-free on anyone rooting for the Steelers but did accomplish the job, as he squeezed the 36-yard attempt inside of the right upright with little room to spare, giving the Steelers their first lead of the game at 12-10 with nine minutes remaining.

Feeling the motivation from finally seizing the lead, the Steelers' defense again made a statement on the following possession. Sensing an opportunity to go for the knockout after Pearson bobbled Gerela's kickoff and had no option other than to fall on it to retain possession, the Steelers attacked the Cowboys from the start of the offensive series. Staubach dropped back to pass from just a few yards in front of his own goal line and zipped a ball over the middle of the field. From out of nowhere Wagner darted in front of it and intercepted the ball in mid stride, breaking furiously for the Dallas end zone and nearly reaching it before being stopped by Cowboys' tackle Ralph Neely near the Dallas 7-yard line. It was yet another in a long line of magnificent and equally timely plays throughout the postseason for the Pittsburgh defense, putting the Steelers on the doorstep of yet another score and the chance to take a commanding lead with just over seven minutes remaining in the game.

The Steelers tried three consecutive times to crack the Dallas defense and reach the end zone via hard-nosed running, but to no avail. Bleier was bottled up on the first down play, and on second down Bradshaw opted to run the ball himself after finding no open receivers in the end zone. He was upended near the one yard line, and on third down the Steelers again failed to break the plane although they nearly met with a much more severe fate. Harris fumbled the ball upon taking contact, but managed to retain possession as it fortuitously popped straight up into the air and landed directly back in his arms as he was falling to the turf while being tackled.

The play lost a yard, making Noll's choice to again call on Gerela rather than go for the touchdown a sound decision, albeit on the surface a somewhat disappointing one. Still, a field goal would stretch the lead to five points and force Dallas to have to find the end zone in the game's final minutes. Gerela was successful on the 18-yard attempt to push the Steelers' advantage to 15-10 with just under seven minutes remaining. As Gerela teed the ball up for the ensuing kickoff the Steelers knew that another solid defensive stand from their unit that had come up so large for them not just on that afternoon but throughout the playoffs could very well be the final charge needed to lay claim to their second Super Bowl victory.

Dallas took possession at their own 24-yard line after Pearson's kick return. The fact that Staubach, a Super Bowl champion and MVP, was entirely capable of bringing The Cowboys back with one giant heave of his right arm was clearly not lost on the Steelers as they dug in across the line of scrimmage. The Cowboys opened with a short swing pass to fullback Robert Newhouse that gained four yards before Furness made the tackle, then on the following play the Steel Curtain came through again to keep the Cowboys on their heels and the momentum of the game's closing minutes in the

Steelers' favor. Dwight White got free from his blocker and had an open lane to Staubach as the Cowboys' quarterback scrambled and backpedaled outside of the pocket. Staubach barely avoided White's grasp but couldn't avoid the second Steeler on the scene, Greenwood, who brought him down for a ten yard loss.

The Cowboys gained some of the lost yardage back on the following play as Staubach dumped a short pass off to running back Charley Young, who motored forward for a moment before being caught by Lambert well short of the first down marker. Beyond making the critical third down stop, the Steelers did something just as key in showing restraint when extra-curricular activities began to brew after the play. Edwards became tangled up with Richards after the Dallas receiver made a below-the-knees block attempt. Knowing how detrimental a penalty could be in that scenario, Wagner came dashing into the fray from several yards away to separate the visibly fuming Edwards from both Richards and an official to preserve the punt situation and give the ball back to the offense with just over four minutes remaining.

The Steelers took over at their own 30-yard line after the kick, and quickly went to Harris on consecutive runs that netted a total of six yards, bringing up another critical third down. And then, in an instant, another dose of all-time Steelers magic happened. Bradshaw dropped back to pass and managed to stay alive just long enough, and release the ball just soon enough before absorbing a crushing hit, to find Swann streaking downfield a step ahead of Washington. He delivered the ball perfectly on target, an arm's reach ahead of Swann where only he could catch it and Washington had no chance of batting it away. As Washington fell helplessly forward while swiping at Swann's back in desperation, number 88 glided into the end zone for a touchdown, practically carrying the entire city of Pittsburgh with him as he secured a 21-10 Steelers lead.

The score stayed that way as Gerela, after coming up big when he needed to on the previous two field goal attempts, inexplicably missed the point after. Nonetheless the Steelers were under three minutes from victory, and moreover they had severely complicated matters for Staubach and the Dallas offense by stretching the lead to where it would require two touchdowns to come back. While the play marked significant celebration for the Steelers it also came at a cost though. Bradshaw showed the poise and toughness of a veteran leader to stand firm in the face of the oncoming rush long enough to deliver the touchdown pass, but afterward paid the price. He had to be helped to the sideline and on to the Steelers' locker room due to the effects of the hit, and in similar fashion to the end of the AFC Championship game, the Steelers would have to rely on Hanratty to take them the rest of the way on offense.

The Cowboys refused to go quietly though. After Gerela's kickoff reached the end zone for a touchback Staubach went to work, moving the offense swiftly as Dallas faced two opponents – the Steelers' defense and the clock. Staubach began the drive with a short, over-the-middle pass to Young for seven yards. Then on second down he rifled a sideline bomb to Drew Pearson that was good for 30 yards and brought the Cowboys into Steelers' territory and, just as importantly, stopped the clock. On the very next play Staubach found the Cowboys' other Pearson, Preston, on the opposite sideline for an 11-yard pickup and another stoppage of time.

Staubach couldn't continue his aerial attack though. On the next play he tried to weave around in the pocket to buy time for his receivers but was ultimately sacked by White at the Steelers' 34-yard line for a two yard loss, setting up second and twelve as the two minute warning timeout commenced. When play resumed, Staubach went for broke and it paid off. He connected with rookie receiver Percy Howard, who had worked free from Blount's coverage, in the front left corner of the end zone for a touchdown. The score injected a level of uncertainty back into the game that just a few moments prior had seemed to be all but secured for the Steelers. Fritsch made the extra point and the Steelers' lead was reduced to 21-17 with one minute and forty five seconds remaining.

Which, quite frankly, is exactly a situation that any team would have gladly accepted when they opened training camp the previous summer. Up four points in the Super Bowl and set to receive the ball with less than two minutes remaining. All that was left for the Steelers to do to bring on the championship celebration was to secure the inevitable Dallas onside kick and then possess the football long enough to allow the final 105 seconds to tick harmlessly away. For any of the 24 other teams not competing in the season's final game as well as for the one standing across the Orange Bowl field, which by that point had become fully-engulfed in late-afternoon shadows, the Steelers' position would absolutely have been an enviable one.

But of course everything is much easier said by the armchair quarterbacks than it is done by the men who lace up the cleats and don the pads. For the Steelers the game's outcome was still very much up in the air as Fritsch teed the ball up for the kickoff. As expected Fritsch dribbled a short rolling kick toward the left side of the field that the Dallas players immediately broke toward in an attempt to recover. The outcome wasn't even close, as Gerry Mullins grabbed it without a Cowboy even being within several feet of him. The Dallas gamble hadn't worked out, and as a result Hanratty came on to lead the Steelers offense for what all involved hoped would end in a victory formation.

But, as with anything worth having, it didn't come quite that easily. Harris was dropped for a loss on the first play of the series by Dallas safety Charlie Waters with help from several of his teammates, after which the Cowboys promptly called a timeout to stop the clock. Harris again got the call on second down but picked up only the yardage he had lost on the previous carry, putting the Steelers in a third and ten scenario.

The Cowboys again used a timeout to stop the clock, and the Steelers' attempt to close out the victory was, for the moment, struggling. In addition to needing the full ten yards for a first down, Dallas also had one more timeout at their disposal.

When play resumed, Bleier carried into the middle of the line for only a yard before being downed by Pugh, and Dallas, as expected, used their last remaining timeout to halt the clock with just under a minute and a half remaining.

Facing a decision, Pittsburgh elected to run a play on fourth down rather than bringing on Walden to punt, which would have brought with it the risk of a Dallas block or a long return. In essence it was a sacrifice of field position by Noll in the name of risk mitigation, and a firm display of confidence in the Pittsburgh defensive unit. Bleier gained only a yard on the run that followed, of course leaving many a Steelers' fan to second guess the strategy. Nonetheless, the Super Bowl was now entirely in the hands of the group that anyone sporting black and gold would want it to be – the Steel Curtain defense.

Staubach faced a bleak, yet not impossible, situation, and opened the Cowboys' last gasp offensive possession in shotgun formation. On first down he took off scrambling after not finding any viable options downfield, and reached midfield before Holmes tackled him. The clock continued to tick down toward one minute remaining, as the Cowboys had sold out on the Steelers' previous offensive series by using all of their remaining timeouts. After the offense hastily lined up for the next play Staubach found Preston Pearson over the middle for an 11-yard gain, but the clock continued rolling below 30 seconds remaining as Kellum made the open field tackle.

The game nearly came to a close on the following play as a hurried Staubach fumbled the shotgun snap, but was able to recover it and free himself from the oncoming Pittsburgh rush long enough to fire downfield toward the end zone. The pass fell incomplete however, stopping the clock with just 12 seconds remaining. The stoppage in play allowed Dallas to better set itself for the next play, but despite their efforts the result was the same. Staubach uncorked a high arching pass to the back right corner of the end zone, the kind so commonly seen in last-ditch attempts from a team trailing at the end of a game. As the ball came down among a combined mass of black and white jerseys, Thomas managed to get a hand on it and swat it away with three seconds remaining.

Three seconds stood between the Steelers and repeat Super Bowl glory. Three more seconds to hold off the ever-dangerous Staubach, three seconds to prevent him from executing another miraculous play like the one he so famously described as a "Hail Mary," which marked the origin of the term being used in a sports context, to beat the Minnesota Vikings in the closing seconds of the divisional round matchup. And in those three seconds indeed came the moment that marked the final nail in the coffin for the Cowboys and solidified the Steelers' standing as the NFL's premier team. The punctuation mark on a hard-fought victory to cap a hard-fought season and first two playoff rounds in defense of their title. The play that elevated the Steelers to the ranks of the NFL's elite in the Super Bowl era and lifted the spirits of black and gold fans from Pittsburgh and beyond.

Staubach fired a deep pass toward the center of the end zone that came down among another collective mass of players from both sides. As everyone watching held their breath in anticipation, Wagner got a hand on the ball to tip it slightly, but it still remained up for grabs. The tension continued for a second longer before an entire fan base could exhale.

That group of course was the Steelers side.

The ball finally fell into Edwards' hands as time expired. With victory sealed, he took off running from the end zone, reaching the Pittsburgh 35-yard line before going down and in turn kicking of the Steelers' opportunity to raise up another piece of championship hardware.

It was a victory that cemented Pittsburgh as the NFL's new dominant franchise. As the 1970's entered their second half the new face of the NFL was unquestionably the Pittsburgh Steelers. It was win that made everyone from young kids to grandmothers swell with pride that their small portion of the map was the epicenter of the football universe, the home of the now back-to-back world champions. What the prior year's Super Bowl victory meant in terms of franchise rebirth, the second meant equally in reinforcement. The Steelers weren't just a flash-in-the-pan winner, a team that caught a break or two in the playoffs and parlayed that into a Super Bowl victory. They had faced down all comers in their title defense, navigated all the battles and quite frankly, won games when they weren't at their best through sheer grit. The 1975 Pittsburgh Steelers were more than just the city's second consecutive championship team. They were, and seemed every bit poised to remain for the foreseeable future, a group that the rest of the NFL indeed was going to have to "deal with."

And while the Steelers reveled in the immediate excitement of becoming repeat champions, there was simply no telling at the time what the larger, broader, more transcendent impact of the victory would become. For as simple logic goes, to get four you have to first get three. And to get three, you have to first get two. And while, on that cool January Florida evening the only thing that truly mattered in the winning locker room was the pride in every player and coach and staff member that simultaneously extended all the way back to the gritty and fiercely loyal fans at home, holding their own celebrations on a much, much colder Pittsburgh evening, history would show that the second Steelers' Super Bowl victory would over time transition from representing a coronation to becoming a lasting cornerstone.

Decades removed, we all know that the glory the Steelers' franchise has achieved across generations didn't stop at two Super Bowl victories, or three, or even that "One for the Thumb" wouldn't stay the Steelers' rallying cry forever, as future eras of the team so rightfully saw to, but rather would be passed along to the crosstown neighbor Penguins. With the benefit of hindsight and the immense privilege, and one glance around the rest of the NFL is indeed all it takes to realize that we're very much privileged to have a franchise that has staked its claim among the small handful of elites over time, we can look back and realize that becoming repeat Super Bowl champions was a critical foundational element of establishing the identity of the Pittsburgh Steelers for years to come.

But at the time, none of that was anything that mattered. What did matter was defending what was so deservedly earned the year prior. What mattered was winning games in spite of nagging injuries and poor weather conditions, because champions find a way to get it done. What mattered, to get right down to it, was Lynn Swann, no, Super Bowl MVP Lynn Swann, making the Dallas defense look like fools all afternoon, ultimately catching the touchdown pass that proved to be the clinching score, when just days before the game every doctor from Miami all the way back to McKeesport said he was a long shot to play.

Maybe George Atkinson was watching. Everyone knows Cliff Harris was.

And as if that wasn't enough to stir the Steeler pride in every black and gold rooting soul then it's for sure worth mentioning that what also mattered was number 12 not budging an inch as he delivered that touchdown pass to

Swann despite what was coming at him head on. The Cowboys may have rung Terry Bradshaw's bell on that particular play, but when it was all over he and his Steelers teammates were was the ones wearing another ring.

All of that mattered as Super Bowl Sunday night turned into the wee hours of Monday morning. But the fact that we're still recalling it over four decades later, the fact that we tell our kids about it and they tell theirs because that's what being a Steelers fan is all about, means that it wasn't just the thrill of that game, that season. It was the story of the process. It was the story of Pittsburgh Steelers football truly becoming Pittsburgh Steelers football.

And, you know – a wise man once said that the thrill isn't just in the winning, it's in the doing.

One More Thing...

Thank you for reading this book; I hope you enjoyed it!

Be sure to check out the rest of the books in the *Black and Gold Dynasty* series to relive all of the Steelers' Super Bowl victories!

And finally, there is one huge favor that I'd ask of you...

Please leave a review of this book wherever you purchased it.

Reviews help other potential readers decide if a book is something they'd be interested in and are a big part of helping authors get visibility on their work.

It doesn't take very long but goes a long way toward helping a book succeed.

Thank you again for reading!

29219978R00050

Printed in Great Britain
by Amazon